A Note to Parents

DK READERS is a compelling program for beginning readers, designed in conjunction with leading literacy experts, including Dr. Linda Gambrell, Professor of Education at Clemson University. Dr. Gambrell has served as President of the National Reading Conference, the College Reading Association, and the International Reading Association.

Beautiful illustrations and superb full-color photographs combine with engaging, easy-to-read stories and informational texts to offer a fresh approach to each subject in the series. Each DK READER is guaranteed to capture a child's interest while developing his or her reading skills, general knowledge, and love of reading.

The five levels of DK READERS are aimed at different reading abilities, enabling you to choose the books that are exactly right for your child:

Pre-level 1: Learning to read
Level 1: Beginning to read
Level 2: Beginning to read alone
Level 3: Reading alone
Level 4: Proficient readers

The "normal" age at which a child begins to read can be anywhere from three to eight years old. Adult participation through the lower levels is very helpful for providing encouragement, discussing storylines, and sounding out unfamiliar words.

No matter which level you select, you can be sure that you are helping your child learn to read, then read to learn!

1

LONDON, NEW YORK,
MELBOURNE, MUNICH, and DELHI

For DK/BradyGames
Global Strategy Guide Publisher
Mike Degler
Digital and Trade Category Publisher
Brian Saliba
Editor-In-Chief
H. Leigh Davis
Operations Manager
Stacey Beheler
Title Manager
Tim Fitzpatrick
Book Designer
Tim Amrhein

For DK Publishing
Publishing Director
Beth Sutinis
Licensing Editor
Nancy Ellwood
Reading Consultant
Linda B. Gambrell, Ph.D.

For WWE
Director, Home Entertainment & Books
Dean Miller
Photo Department
Frank Vitucci, Joshua Tottenham, Jamie Nelsen
Copy Editor Kevin Caldwell
Legal Lauren Dienes-Middlen

DK/BradyGAMES
800 East 96th St., 3rd floor
Indianapolis, IN 46240

11 12 13 10 11 10 9 8 7 6 5 4 3 2

A catalog record for this book is available from the Library of Congress.

ISBN: 978-0-7566-7607-0 (Paperback)

ISBN: 978-0-7566-8698-7 (Hardback)

Printed and bound by Lake Book Manufacturing, Inc.

The publisher would like to thank the following for their kind
permission to reproduce their photographs:
All photos courtesy WWE Entertainment, Inc.
All other images © Dorling Kindersley
For further information see: www.dkimages.com

Discover more at

www.dk.com

Contents

Big Show®

Written by Kevin Sullivan

DK
DK Publishing

Not-So-Little Show

As a youngster, Big Show wasn't like
other children his age. He was always
much bigger and stronger, which caused
many people to stare at the oversized
boy. His great size also made him an all-
star athlete, particularly in basketball.
Despite his success on the court, Big
Show dreamed of one day stepping
inside a wrestling ring and becoming
just like the massive heroes he
watched on television.

Realizing he needed proper
training to perform the dangerous
moves of a professional wrestler,
Big Show turned to Larry Sharpe
for guidance.

As a former wrestler, Sharpe taught the giant basic moves every pro needs to know. After only a few months of training, Big Show caught the attention of major wrestling promotion WCW.

Early Success

In most cases, an in-ring career takes off only after several years of training. But because of his size, Big Show was ready to make his first professional appearance after only a few months of working out at WCW's Power Plant.

Known then as "The Giant," Big Show's first order of business was to face WCW Champion Hulk Hogan. Going toe to toe with The Hulkster was a brave move for somebody with so little experience. Big Show wasn't afraid of the champ. In fact, he even defeated Hogan for the WCW Title at *Halloween Havoc* in October 1995.

Big Show's Stats
- **Height:** 7' (2.13 m)
- **Weight:** 485 lbs. (220 kg)
- **From:** Tampa, FL
- **Signature Moves:** Chokeslam, Cobra Clutch Backbreaker

Over the next several years, Big Show proved his dominance over WCW's Superstars, including Randy Savage and Kevin Nash. He also beat the legendary Ric Flair in April 1996 to become a two-time WCW Champion.

Instant Impact

After nearly four years of competing for WCW, Big Show jumped to rival WWE in February 1999. During Mr. McMahon's Steel Cage Match with Stone Cold Steve Austin at *St. Valentine's Day Massacre*, the giant newcomer tore through the bottom of the ring and attacked fan favorite Austin.

Big Show used his size advantage to toss Stone Cold straight through the steel structure.

It was the first time WWE fans had ever seen Big Show in one of their rings, and his impact was clear.

Big Show then became an important part of Mr. McMahon's evil group called The Corporation. Big Show served as the bodyguard, and he was responsible for making sure The Rock kept his WWE Championship at *WrestleMania XV*. Unfortunately for McMahon and The Rock, things didn't go as planned. In a fit of rage, McMahon blamed Big Show for the foiled plan and even slapped the massive Superstar across the face. Big Show responded by punching the boss, making the WWE newcomer an instant fan favorite.

At *Survivor Series* in November 1999, Stone Cold Steve Austin was scheduled to compete against Triple H and The Rock. However, Austin was struck down by a car before the event. Big Show was chosen to compete in his place. It was just the opening Big Show needed to put an exclamation point on his first year with WWE.

Heading into the match, Triple H and The Rock expected Stone Cold to be the third competitor. When Big Show was announced, both Superstars were greatly shocked. They had to change their game plan for a man several hundred pounds heavier than Austin. Big Show was too much for them to handle.

He won the match and the WWE
Championship after hitting Triple H
with a bone-crushing Chokeslam move.
Big Show's victory put him in very
strong company. Prior to his win,
only Buddy Rogers, Ric Flair, Hulk
Hogan, Randy Savage, and Kevin
Nash had captured both the WWE
and WCW/NWA Championships.

Making a Change

As WWE Champion, Big Show made quick work of Big Boss Man at *Armageddon* 1999. He then lost the title back to Triple H in January 2000. Eager to get the title around his waist once again, Big Show earned a spot in the main event of *WrestleMania 2000*.

There, he competed against Triple H, The Rock, and Mick Foley. Unfortunately, Big Show could not regain the gold at *WrestleMania*. The loss was tough for the former champ to accept, and his career soon began to sink to new lows. Rather than competing in main events as the mighty Big Show, he started to impersonate past and present Superstars, such as Hulk Hogan, Val Venis, and Rikishi. The impersonations made WWE audiences laugh, but it was clear that they would not lead Big Show back to the WWE Championship. Realizing that he needed to make a change, Big Show soon disappeared from WWE so he could work at regaining his championship form.

New and Improved

Big Show returned with renewed dedication at the 2001 *Royal Rumble*. Proving he was back in a big way, he captured the Hardcore Championship on three separate occasions. However, it wasn't until late 2002 that he truly regained his main-event status.

After being traded from *Raw* to *SmackDown* in October, Big Show easily destroyed many top names, including Matt Hardy and Rikishi. He then set his sights on Brock Lesnar and the WWE Championship. The two Superstars squared off at *Survivor Series*. It looked like Lesnar would walk away with the win after he hit Big Show with a devastating F5 move.

However, before the referee could finish
the count, Lesnar's manager Paul
Heyman shockingly interfered to help
Big Show. With the match's momentum
shifted, Show Chokeslammed Lesnar
onto a steel chair for the win and his
second WWE Championship.

With Heyman on his side and the WWE Championship back around his waist, Big Show displayed a level of rage he had never shown in the past. He even tried to attack former Women's Champion and senior citizen Fabulous Moolah.

The champ's actions toward Moolah didn't sit well with Lesnar, who was still upset about losing the title. He attacked Big Show from behind and sent him through the announcers' table. That wasn't enough payback for Lesnar. He later jumped Big Show from behind again at *Armageddon* 2002. This time, the attack cost Big Show his WWE Championship, as Kurt Angle easily covered the big man for the win.

A Mass of Humanity

Unlike the first time he lost the WWE Championship, Big Show kept his headliner status after *Armageddon.* Over the next several months, he competed in several high-profile matches against the best *SmackDown* had to offer, including Undertaker and Rey Mysterio.

In October 2003, Big Show returned to championship form when he defeated Eddie Guerrero for the coveted United States Championship at *No Mercy.*

He proudly held the title for five months before losing it to John Cena at Madison Square Garden in the opening match of *WrestleMania XX.*

Shortly after the loss, Big Show made a big mistake—he promised to quit WWE if he couldn't beat Eddie Guerrero. Unfortunately, he did not defeat Guerrero. This forced the giant Superstar to leave the only career he had ever known. Luckily, he wasn't gone for long. After five months away from the ring, the giant made a shocking return, attacking nearly the entire *SmackDown* lineup during a Lumberjack Match in September 2004. He left a pile of fallen bodies in the ring.

Sports-Entertainment's Crown Jewel

Over his career, Big Show has competed in some of the most memorable *WrestleMania* matches. One of his best-known encounters saw him battle in a Sumo Match against the 6' 8" (2.03 m), 508-pound (230 kg) grand sumo champion Akebono at *WrestleMania 21.*

Wearing a traditional mawashi, Big Show nearly defeated the sumo legend. In the end, the WWE Superstar was out of his element and eventually fell to the mighty Akebono.

What is a Mawashi?

A mawashi is the belt that sumo wrestlers wear during competition. Made from 30 feet of silk, the mawashi is wrapped around the wrestler's waist and is often used by his opponent as a way to gain leverage.

Monsters of Raw

Big Show was drafted back to *Raw* in June 2005. After handily defeating Snitsky on several occasions, he formed a frightening alliance with Kane. Together, the massive duo defeated Trevor Murdoch and Lance Cade for the World Tag Team Championship at *Taboo Tuesday* in November 2005.

For the rest of the year, many of *Raw*'s greatest tag teams tried to dethrone Big Show and Kane, but none could defeat them. Show and Kane even beat many *SmackDown* teams, including tag champs Batista and Rey Mysterio at *Armageddon*.

Big Show and Kane turned back Carlito and Chris Masters at *WrestleMania 22*, leaving many to believe the pair would never lose the gold. Just one night later on *Raw*, Kenny and Mikey of the Spirit Squad surprisingly defeated them.

Hoping to regain the gold, Big Show and Kane quickly challenged the Spirit Squad to a rematch for the World Tag Team Championship.

Many believed they would simply squash the new champs. During the contest, Kane began to act very strangely. In a crazed fit of rage, he started throwing chairs into the ring. He even chokeslammed the referee after he tried to pull one of the chairs away. Hoping to calm the savage beast, Big Show tried to reason with his partner. Kane didn't want to hear it. Instead, he chokeslammed Show, marking the end of their partnership.

Championships Big Show has Held
- WWE Championship
- United States Championship
- World Tag Team Championship
- WWE Tag Team Championship
- WWE Hardcore Championship
- ECW Championship
- WCW Championship
- WCW Tag Team Championship

Extreme Giant

ECW was popular in sports-entertainment during the 1990s. However, money problems forced the company to close its doors in 2001. After ECW closed, its Superstars occasionally appeared on WWE TV until 2006, when ECW returned fulltime alongside *Raw* and *SmackDown*.

To celebrate ECW's return, a special WWE vs. ECW Battle Royal was held in Dayton, Ohio. Hoping to prove their dominance, WWE sent many of their best Superstars, including Edge, Matt Hardy, and Big Show. Little did WWE know that Big Show wasn't really on their side. Instead of helping his team win the match, he turned on WWE to join forces with ECW.

ECW Superstars were always known for their toughness, but they were no match for the newest member of their roster. Within days of joining ECW, Big Show tore through many of ECW's top names, including Tommy Dreamer and Super Crazy.

On July 4, 2006, Big Show won ECW's top prize when he defeated Rob Van Dam for the ECW Championship. The win made Show the only Superstar in history to win the WCW, WWE, and ECW championships.

As champion, Big Show had a giant target on his back in the eyes of the ECW Originals. They felt that only Superstars who competed for the organization in the 1990s should carry the title. Former ECW Champion Sabu led the charge of Originals hoping to get back the gold. Despite many opportunities, he never did wrest the title away from the mighty champion.

Big Show proudly carried the ECW Championship into late 2006, when he took part in one of sports-entertainment history's biggest matches.

At *Cyber Sunday*, he stepped into the ring against World Heavyweight Champion King Booker and WWE Champion John Cena. This would be a rare Champion of Champions Match. In the end, Booker pinned Cena after hitting him with his championship.

The loss was the first major blemish in Big Show's lengthy ECW reign. It marked the beginning of a lengthy string of bad luck. At *Survivor Series*, he captained a team of Superstars that lost to John Cena's squad. At *December to Dismember*, he finally lost the ECW Championship to Bobby Lashley in an Extreme Elimination Chamber Match.

Boxer versus Superstar

Following his loss at *December to Dismember*, Big Show disappeared from WWE. After more than a year away, many fans believed they had seen the last of the big man. At *No Way Out* in February 2008, Big Show made a surprise appearance, which eventually led to another epic *WrestleMania* match.

After announcing he was back and better than ever, Big Show tried to make an example of the much smaller Rey Mysterio by picking him up for a chokeslam. Before Show could drop Mysterio to the mat, famed boxer Floyd "Money" Mayweather ran into the ring to make the save.

The boxer then nailed Big Show with several punches to the face, which ultimately broke his nose. After the attack, both men agreed to settle their differences at *WrestleMania XXIV*.

Under the stars at Florida's Citrus Bowl stadium, the monstrous Big Show squared off against the 5' 8" (1.73 m) Floyd Mayweather in a classic David-versus-Goliath matchup. As expected, Big Show manhandled his smaller opponent for much of the match. Despite his strong showing, the big man eventually fell to Mayweather after the boxer nailed him with a pair of brass knuckles.

Big Show's *WrestleMania* Opponents

WrestleMania XV	Mankind
WrestleMania 2000	Triple H, The Rock, and Mick Foley
WrestleMania X-Seven	Kane and Raven
WrestleMania XIX (with A-Train)	Undertaker
WrestleMania XX	John Cena
WrestleMania 21	Akebono
WrestleMania 22 (with Kane)	Carlito and Chris Masters
WrestleMania XXIV	Floyd Mayweather
WrestleMania XXV	John Cena and Edge
WrestleMania XXVI (with The Miz)	John Morrison and R-Truth

Battle of the Big Men

Every WWE Superstar wants to be seen as the biggest and baddest on the roster. In February 2008, The Great Khali felt that Big Show's return to the ring threatened his role as the biggest, so he attacked the returning Superstar on an episode of *SmackDown*. The assault only angered Big Show, who proved he was WWE's ultimate giant when he beat Khali with a chokeslam at *Backlash*.

Despite Big Show's convincing victory over The Great Khali, WWE's other big men lined up to take on the giant. Mark Henry, Kane, Vladimir Kozlov, and several others tried. Like The Great Khali before them, they all fell short in their attempt to chop Big Show down to size.

No one could slow him down until
he ran into Undertaker. After defeating
the "Phenom" at *No Mercy*, Big Show
lost to Undertaker three straight times,
including a Casket Match at
Survivor Series.

Big Show rebounded well from his
Undertaker setback and picked up
several big wins, including one over
Triple H on *SmackDown*. Because of his
great success, Show was rewarded with
a World Heavyweight Championship
Match against John Cena and Edge at
WrestleMania XXV.

The match was the latest in a long line
of high-profile *WrestleMania* matches
for Big Show. Unfortunately, he did not
walk away with the win. Cena won the
match after hitting both Edge and Big
Show with the Attitude Adjustment.

Tag Team Dominance

When Chris Jericho's tag team partner, Edge, went down with an injury, he chose the biggest replacement he could find: Big Show. Luckily for Show, Y2J was already one half of the Unified Tag Team Champions. This meant Big Show became the other half of the champion team simply by being named as Edge's replacement. Together, Jericho and Big Show held the title for nearly five months and beat many top teams, including Cryme Tyme and the pairing of Batista and Rey Mysterio. It wasn't until the *WWE TLC* pay-per-view in December 2009 that they lost the gold to Triple H and Shawn Michaels.

As a result of their winning ways, Jericho and Big Show were named the 2009 Tag Team of the Year at the Slammy Awards. Unfortunately, though, the end of the road was near for the successful duo. Shortly after receiving the award, Y2J was forced to leave *Raw* when he and Big Show lost their rematch with Triple H and HBK.

While Jericho pouted over leaving *Raw*, Big Show was busy scouting his next tag team partner. He eventually settled on The Miz, who proved to be just as valuable as Y2J. In February 2010, Big Show and Miz captured the Unified Tag Team Championship when they beat the tandem of CM Punk and Luke Gallows, as well as Triple H and HBK in a Triple Threat Elimination Match on *Raw*.

Notable Big Show Tag Team Partners
- Lex Luger (1997)
- Sting (1998)
- Scott Hall (1998)
- Undertaker (1999)
- Kane (2005)
- Chris Jericho (2009)
- The Miz (2010)

Knockout

After a while, The Miz's ego became too much for Big Show to tolerate. Immediately after losing the Unified Tag Team Championship to The Hart Dynasty in April 2010, Big Show flattened his annoying partner with a forceful right hand. This ended their partnership. The giant Superstar was then drafted to *SmackDown*, where fans adored him for punishing The Miz.

Big Show refused to make his way slowly up the *SmackDown* ladder. Instead, he forced his way to the top and challenged World Heavyweight Champion Jack Swagger. The two Superstars battled at the *Over the Limit* event, with Big Show dominating most of the contest.

Fearing he would lose his title to his overpowering opponent, Swagger intentionally got himself disqualified. This greatly angered Big Show, who punched the champ out cold before finally going back to the locker room.

For years, nearly every WWE Superstar has feared Big Show's powerful knockout punch. That's why CM Punk and his Straight Edge Society attempted to weaken the punch's impact by attacking Big Show's hand with the steel ring steps. The assault would have sidelined a normal man, but not Big Show. He ignored the pain and went on to defeat CM Punk, Luke Gallows, and Joseph Mercury in a 3-on-1 Handicap Match at *SummerSlam*.

Big Show's victory was just the latest example of his size, strength, and determination being too much for WWE to handle. For more than 15 years, countless Superstars, have tried to stop the mammoth force.

Opponents included Hall of Famers Hulk Hogan and Ric Flair. None has put him down. Clearly, Big Show is a force unlike any other, and when he finally decides to retire, he will go down in history as one of the greatest of all time.

Glossary

Alliance
Agreement, pact, partnership

Assault
Physical attack, beating

Coveted
Desired, hoped for

Dedication
Commitment, devotion

Determination
Willpower, insistence, resolve

Disqualified
Prohibited, banned, barred, not qualified

Dominance
Power, authority, control, superiority

Element
An environment suited to an individual person

Headliner
Main performer in a show or event, star of the show

High-Profile
Prestigious, glamorous, high-status

Impersonate
Imitate, mimic, pretend to be

Leverage
Influence, control, mechanical advantage

Mammoth
Huge, enormous, giant

Manhandle
Push, shove, jostle, physically force

Rebound
Bounce back, return

Rival
Competitor, opponent, enemy

Roster
List, catalog, inventory, record

Savage
Violent, brutal, wild

Senior Citizen
An elderly person, someone of retirement age or older

Signature Move
A move that a Superstar specializes in performing

Tandem
A team of two people, a pair, a duo

Title
A championship, or the belt or trophy awarded for winning a championship

Tolerate
Put up with, allow, endure

Ultimately
Eventually, in the end, finally